EASY PIANO

 # ONE DIRECTION

UP ALL NIGHT

T0070553

ISBN 978-1-4803-6909-2

7777 W. BLUEMOUND RD. P.O. BOX 13819 MILWAUKEE, WI 53213

Visit Hal Leonard Online at
www.halleonard.com

WHAT MAKES YOU BEAUTIFUL

Words and Music by SAVAN KOTECHA,
RAMI YACOUB and CARL FALK

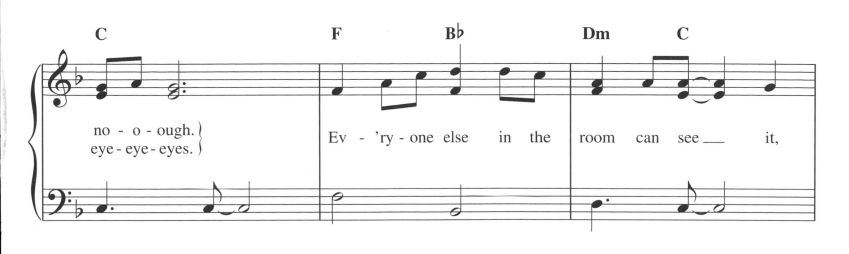

no - o - ough.
eye - eye - eyes.
Ev - 'ry - one else in the room can see __ it,

ev - 'ry - one else but __ you, ooh. __ Ba - by, you

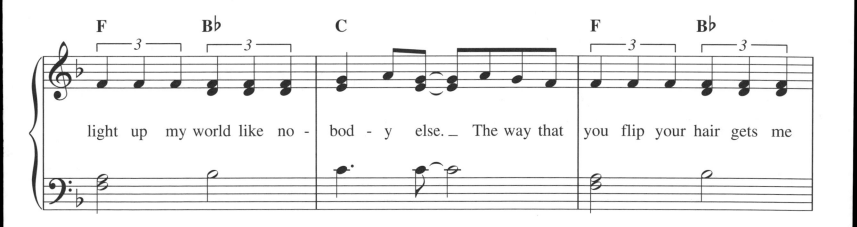

light up my world like no - bod - y else. _ The way that you flip your hair gets me

o - ver - whelmed. _ But when you smile at the ground, it ain't

4

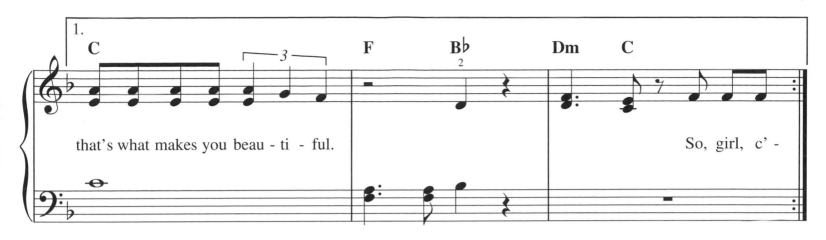

1.

that's what makes you beau - ti - ful.   So, girl, c' -

2.

that's what makes you beau - ti - ful.   Na, na, na, na, na, na, na, na, ___ na.

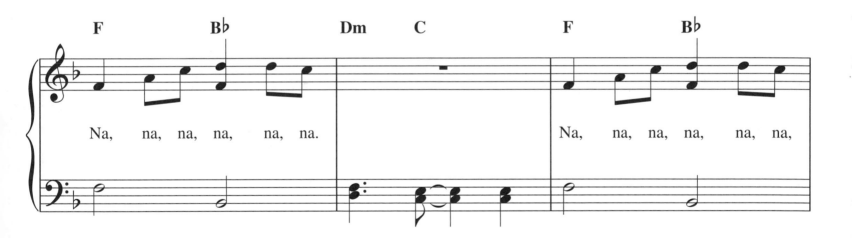

Na, na, na, na, na, na.   Na, na, na, na, na, na,

na, na, ___ na.   Na, na, na, na, na, na.   Ba - by, you

you flip your hair gets me o - ver - whelmed. But when you
stand why I want you so des - p'rate - ly. Right now I'm

smile at the ground, it ain't hard to tell you don't
look - ing at you and I can't be - lieve you don't

know - oh - oh, you don't know you're beau - ti - ful. Oh - oh - oh,
know - oh - oh, you don't know you're beau - ti - ful.

you don't know you're beau - ti - ful. Oh - oh - oh, that's what makes you beau - ti - ful.

GOTTA BE YOU

Words and Music by STEVE MAC
and AUGUST RIGO

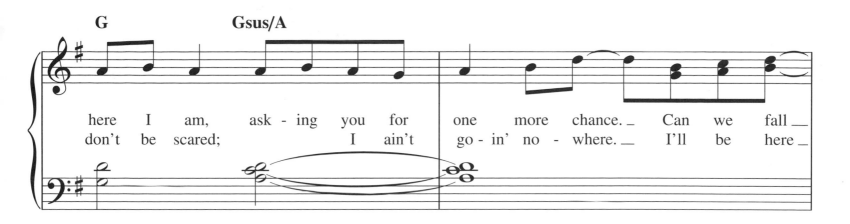

here I am, ask-ing you for one more chance. _ Can we fall _
don't be scared; I ain't go-in' no - where. _ I'll be here _

_ one more time, _ stop the tape _ and re - wind? _
_ by your side; _ no more fears, _ no more cry'n. _

_ And if you walk a-way, I _ know _ I'll _ fade, _ 'cause there is
_ But if you

no - bod - y else. _ It's got - ta be you,

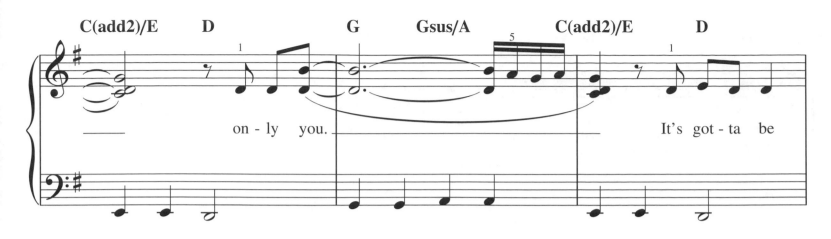

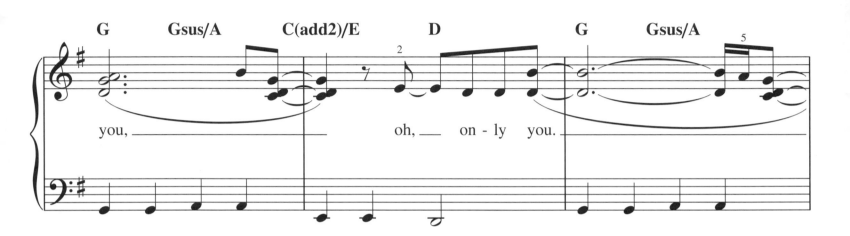

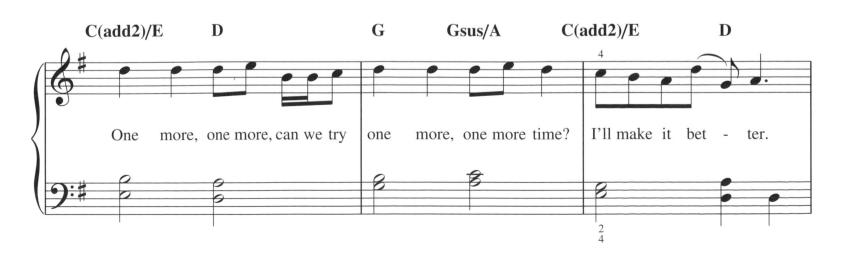

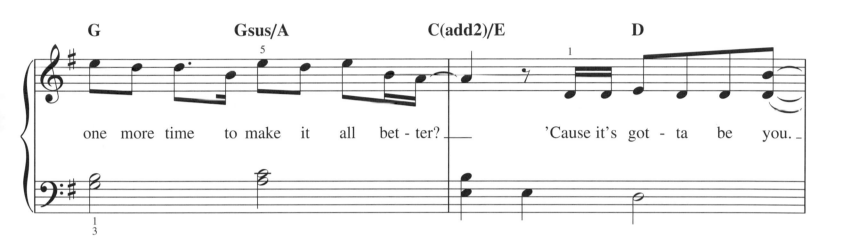

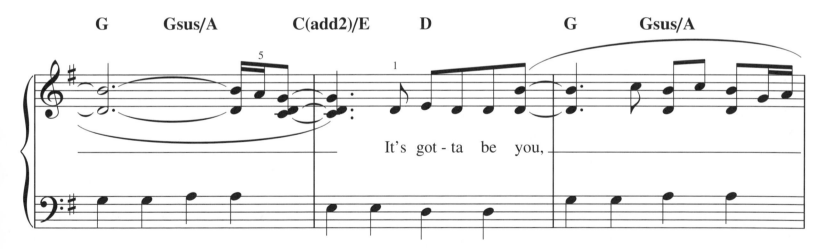

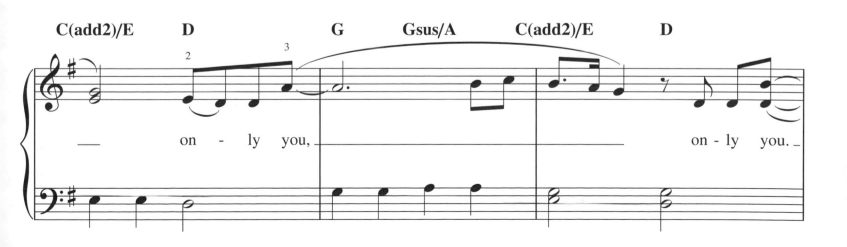

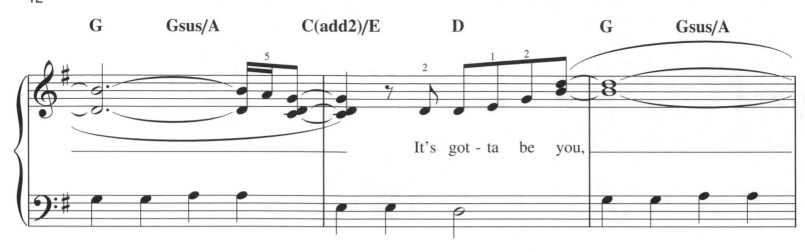

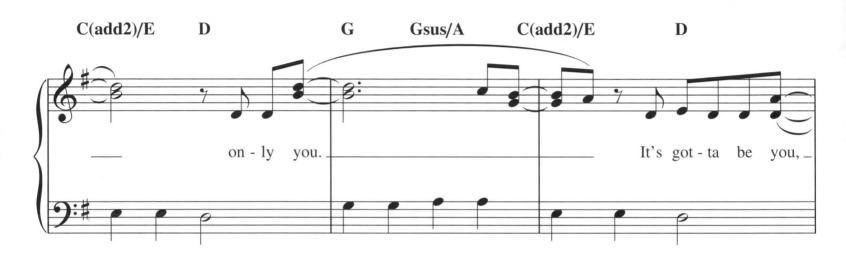

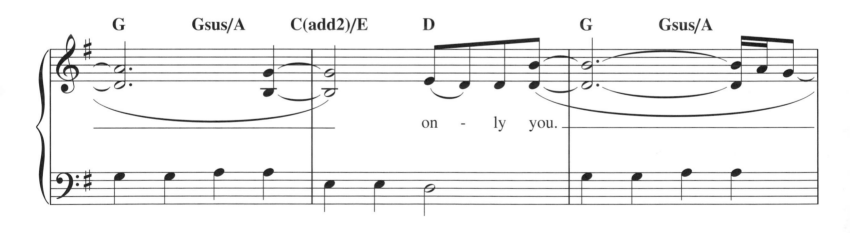

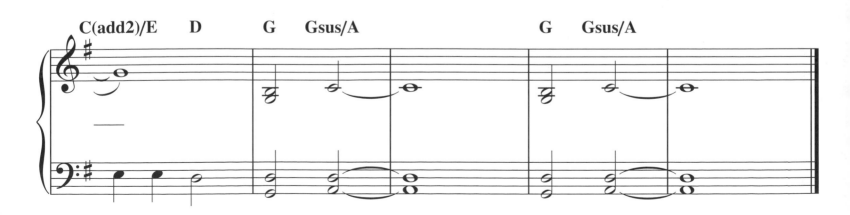

ONE THING

Words and Music by SAVAN KOTECHA,
CARL FALK and RAMI YACOUB

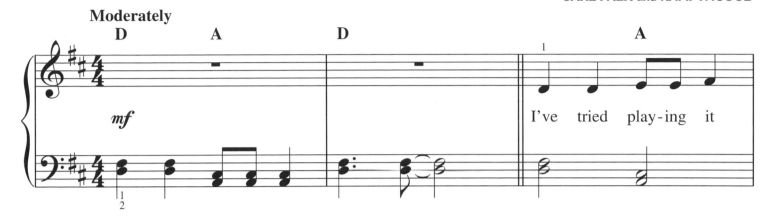

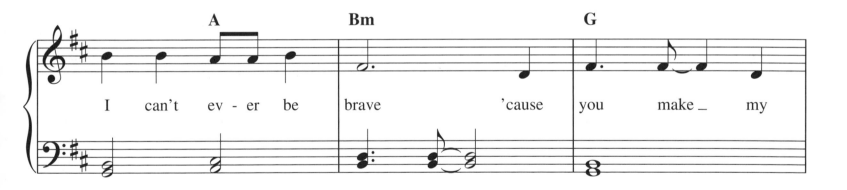

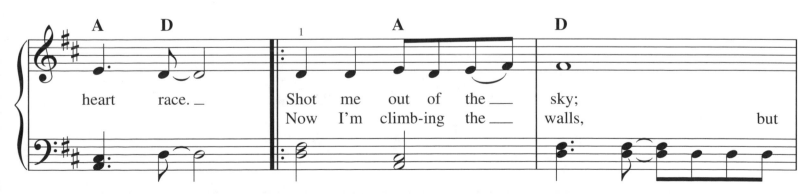

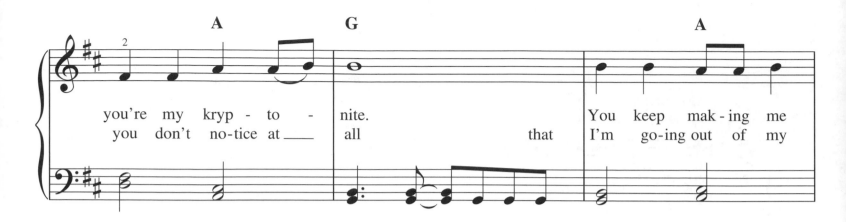

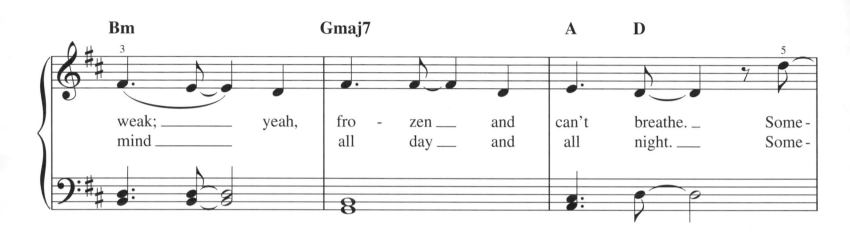

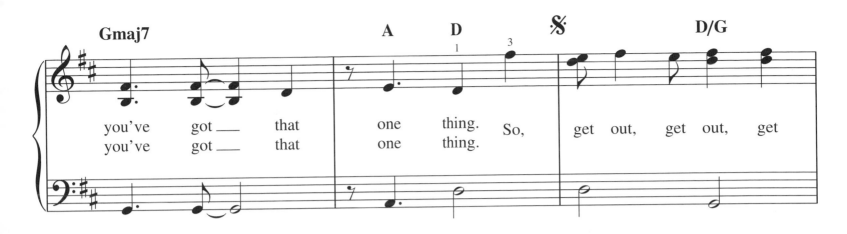

you've got ___ that one thing. So, get out, get out, get
you've got ___ that one thing.

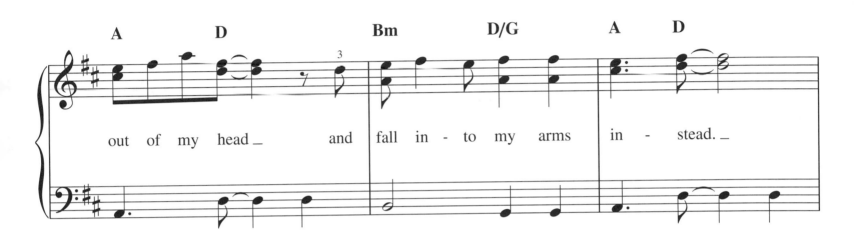

out of my head ___ and fall in-to my arms in - stead. ___

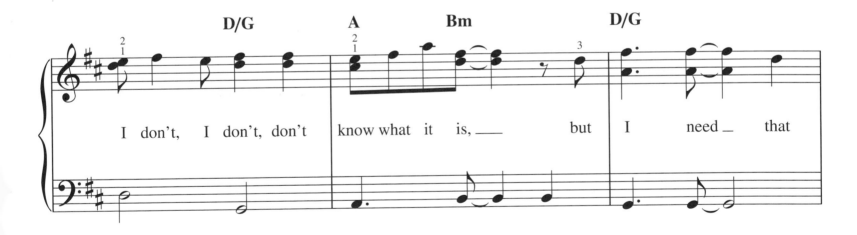

I don't, I don't, don't know what it is, ___ but I need ___ that

one thing, ___ and you've got ___ that one thing.

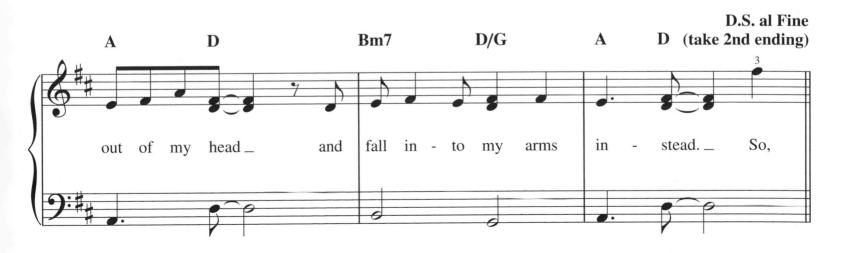

MORE THAN THIS

Words and Music by
JAMIE SCOTT

I'm bro - ken; do you hear me?
If I'm loud - er, would you see me?

I'm blind - ed, 'cause you are ev - 'ry-thing I see. I'm danc - ing
Would you lay down in my arms and res - cue me? 'Cause we are

a - lone, and I'm pray - ing that your heart will just turn a - round.
the same. You save me, but when you leave, it's gone a - gain.

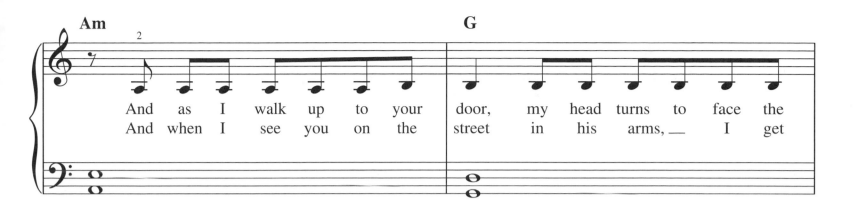

And as I walk up to your door, my head turns to face the
And when I see you on the street in his arms, ___ I get

floor, 'cause I can't look you in the eyes and say: ___
weak. My bod - y fails; I'm on my knees, pray - ing: ___

When he

o - pens his arms ___ and holds you close to - night, ___ it just won't feel ___ right, _

'cause I can love you more than this. Yeah. _ When he lays you down, _ I might just die ___ in-

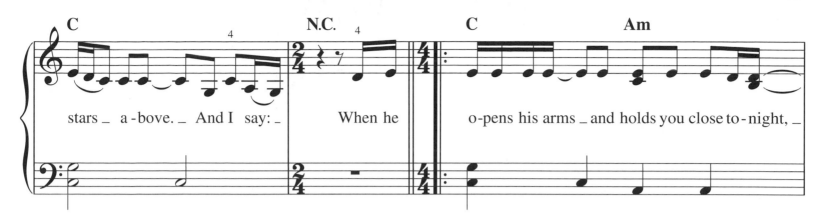

stars _ a-bove. _ And I say: _ When he o-pens his arms _ and holds you close to-night, _

_____ it just won't feel _ right, _ 'cause I can love you more than this. Yeah. _ When he

lays you down, _ I might just die in-side; it just don't feel _ right, _ 'cause I can love you more than

1.
this, yeah. _ When he

2.
this, can love _ you more than this.

UP ALL NIGHT

Words and Music by SAVAN KOTECHA
and MATT SQUIRE

Moderately fast

It feels like we've been liv - ing in fast - for - ward;
Don't e - ven care a - bout the ta - ble break - ing;

an - oth - er mo - ment pass - ing by. The par - ty's end - ing, but it's
we on - ly wan - na have a laugh. I'm on - ly think - ing 'bout this

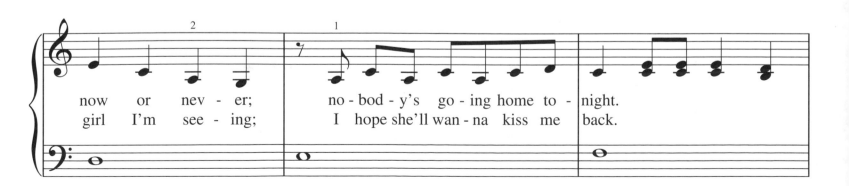

now or nev - er; no - bod - y's go - ing home to - night.
girl I'm see - ing; I hope she'll wan - na kiss me back.

Ka - ty Per-ry's on re - play, _ she's on re - play. _ D - J got the floor to shake, _

the floor to shake. _ Peo-ple go-ing all the way, _ yeah, all the way. _

I'm still wide a - wake. _ I wan-na stay up all night and jump _

_ a - round _ un-til _ we see _ the sun. _ I wan-na stay

up all night and find ___ a girl __ and tell ___ her she's _ the one. ___ Hold on to the feel-

- ing and don't let it go, ___ 'cause we got the floor ___ now. Get out of con-trol! ___ I wan-na stay

up all night and do ___ it all __ with you. ___ Up all

To Coda ⊕

night like this, all night. _ Up all night like this, all night. _

C **G** **F**

Ka-ty Per-ry's on re-play, __ she's on re-play. __ We're gon-na wan-na stay __
D-J got the floor to shake, __ the floor to shake. __

G **C**

up all night. Up all night, up all night,

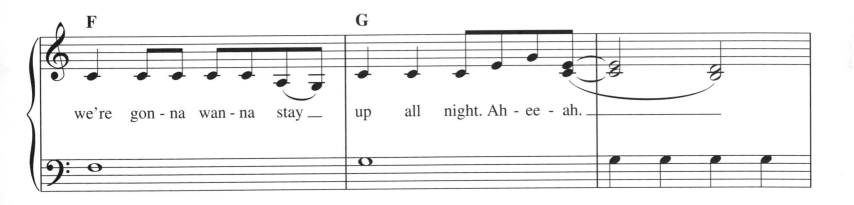

F **G**

we're gon-na wan-na stay __ up all night. Ah - ee - ah. ____

D.S. al Coda

I wan-na stay

CODA

night. __ Up all night.

I WISH

Words and Music by SAVAN KOTECHA,
CARL FALK and RAMI YACOUB

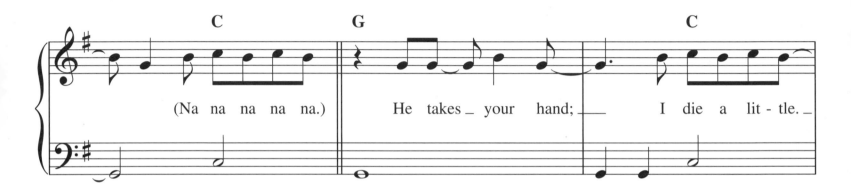

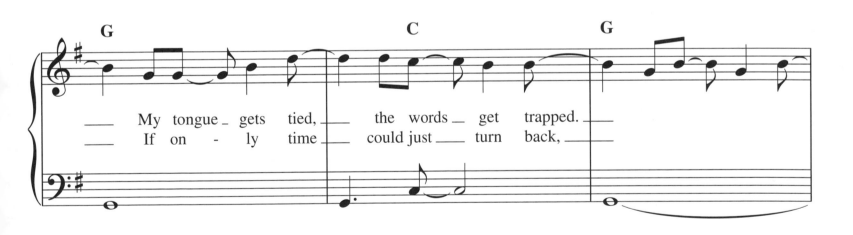

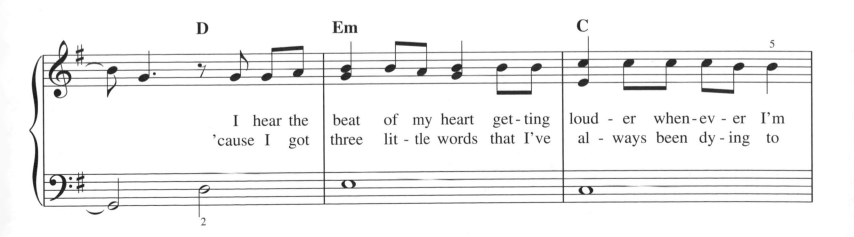

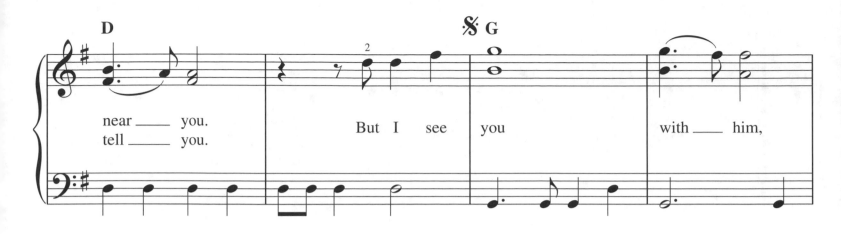

near _____ you.
tell _____ you.

But I see you

with ___ him,

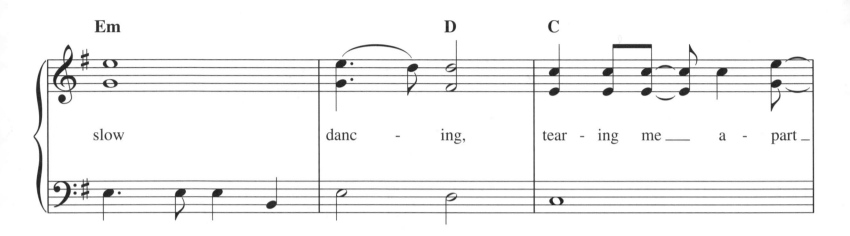

slow

danc - ing,

tear - ing me ___ a - part ___

___ 'cause you ___ don't see. ___

When - ev - er

To Coda ⊕

you

kiss ___ him,

I'm

break - ing.

on   'cause you wan - na say   good - night.   'Cause I   see

you   with _____ him,   slow

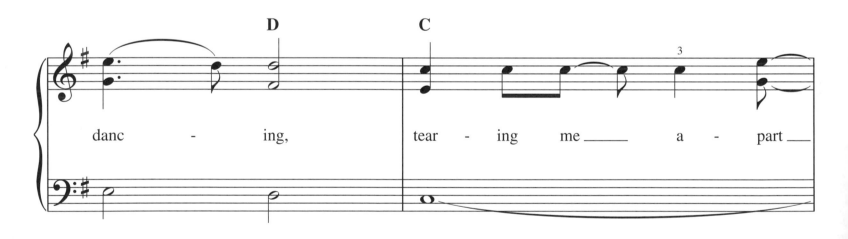

danc -   ing,   tear - ing me ___ a - part ___

D.S. al Coda

___ 'cause you ___ don't   see. ___   But I   see

CODA

Oh,   how   I   wish,   oh,   how   I

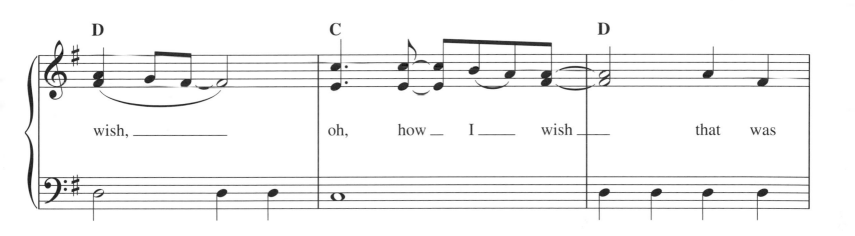

wish, _____   oh,   how I wish _____   that   was

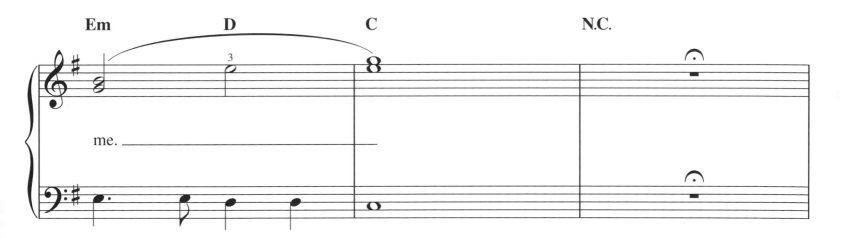

me. _____

Oh,   how I   wish _____   that   was   me.

TELL ME A LIE

Words and Music by TOM MEREDITH,
KELLY CLARKSON and SHEPPARD SOLOMON

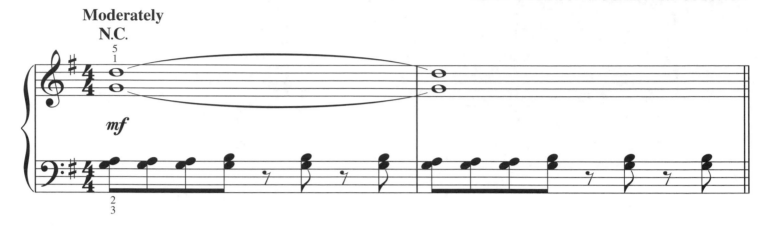

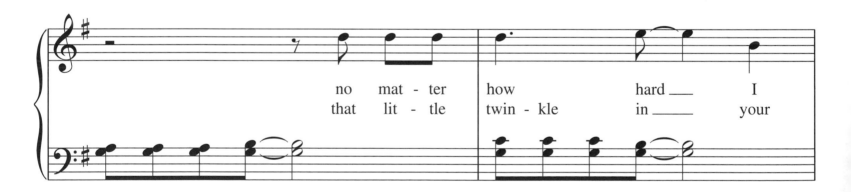

Can't ev-er get it right, ___
Well, you're the charm - ing type; ___

no mat - ter how hard ___ I
that lit - tle twin - kle in ___ your

try, and I've tried. ___
eye gets me ev - 'ry time. ___

Well, I put
And, well, there

up a good fight, _
must have been a time _

but your words cut _ like
I was the rea-son for _ that

knives,
smile.

and I'm tired. _
Keep in mind, _

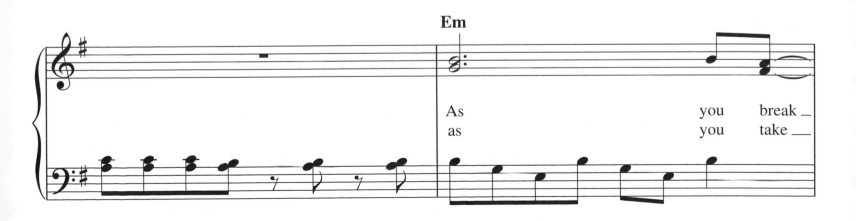

As
as

you break _
you take _

my heart ___ a - gain ___ this
what's left ___ of you ___ and

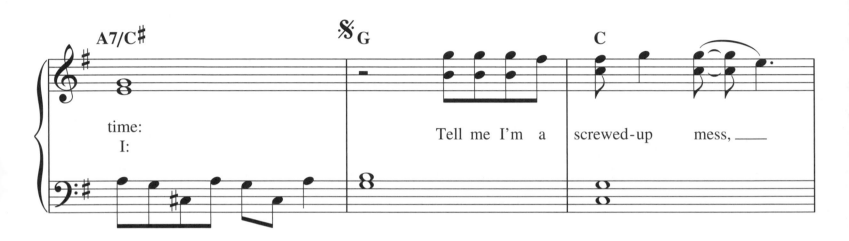

time:
I:

Tell me I'm a screwed-up mess, ___

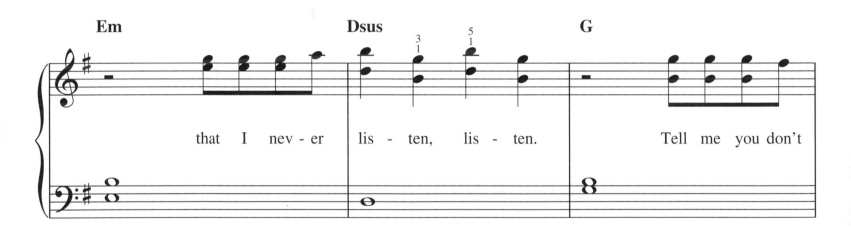

that I nev - er lis - ten, lis - ten.

Tell me you don't

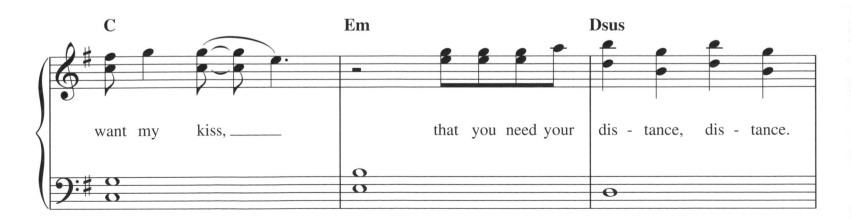

want my kiss, ___

that you need your dis - tance, dis - tance.

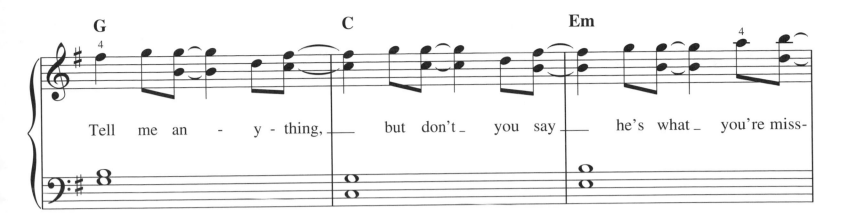

Tell me an-y-thing,___ but don't__ you say___ he's what__ you're miss-

-ing, ba-by. If he's the rea-son that you're leav-ing me to-night,___

spare me what you think__ and tell me a lie.___

tell me a lie.___

36

Tell me a lie.____   Tell me a lie.__

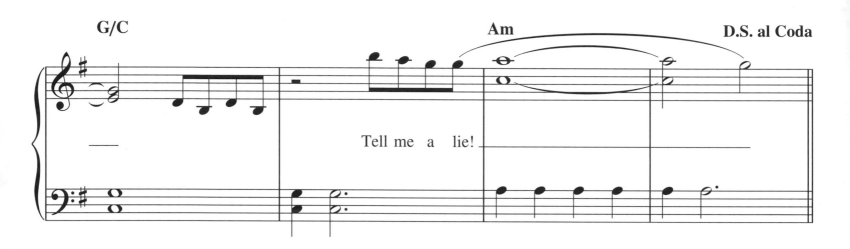

G/C   Am   D.S. al Coda

Tell me a lie!____

CODA

Dsus   G   C

tell me a lie.__   Tell me a lie.__

Em   D   G

Tell me a lie.__

TAKEN

Words and Music by TOBY GAD,
LINDY ROBBINS, NIALL HORAN,
LIAM PAYNE, LOUIS TOMLINSON,
ZAIN MALIK and EDWARD STYLES

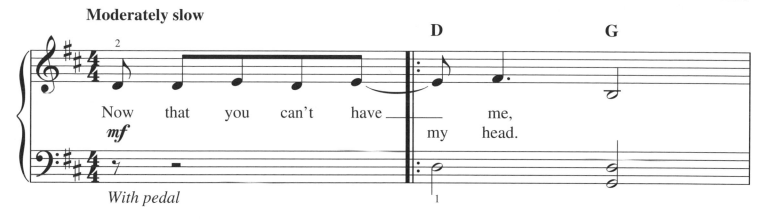

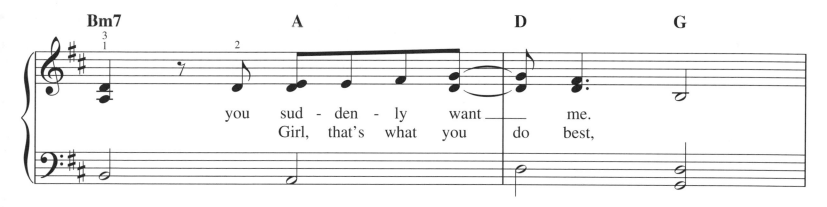

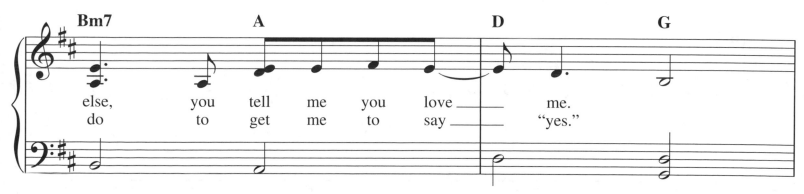

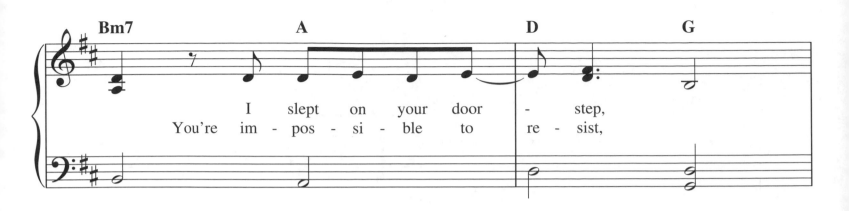

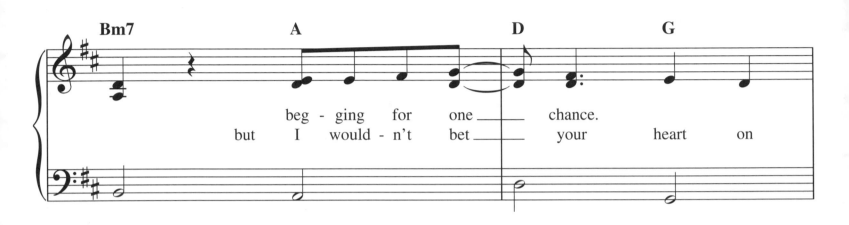

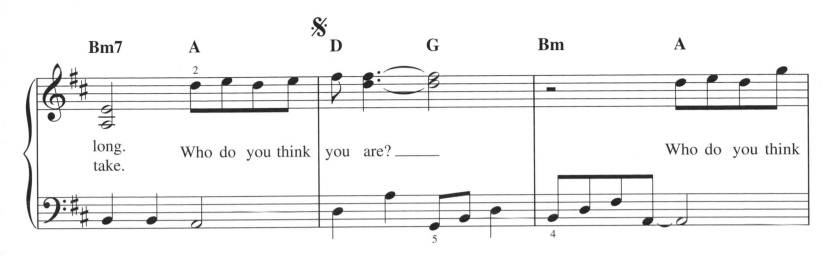

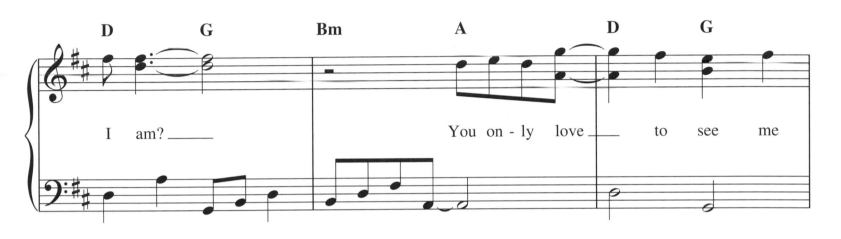

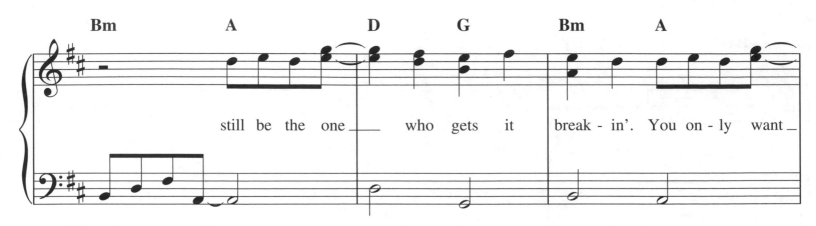

still be the one ___ who gets it break - in'. You on - ly want ___

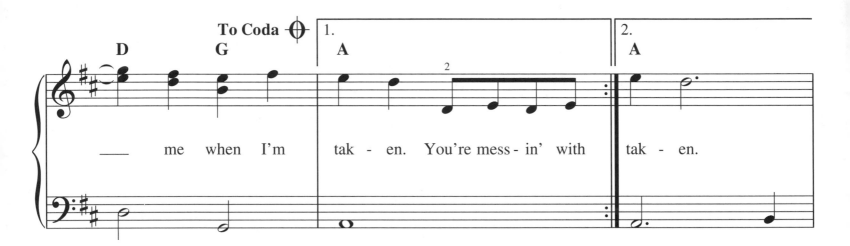

___ me when I'm tak - en. You're mess - in' with tak - en.

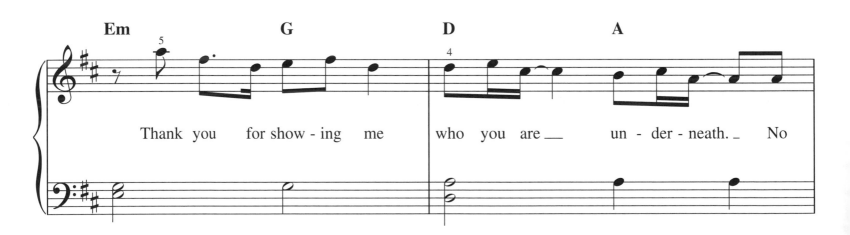

Thank you for show - ing me who you are ___ un - der - neath. ___ No

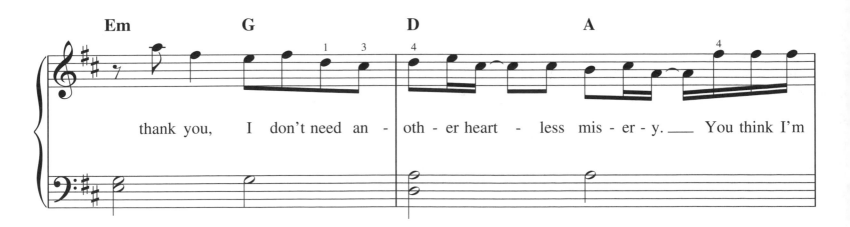

thank you, I don't need an - oth - er heart - less mis - er - y. ___ You think I'm

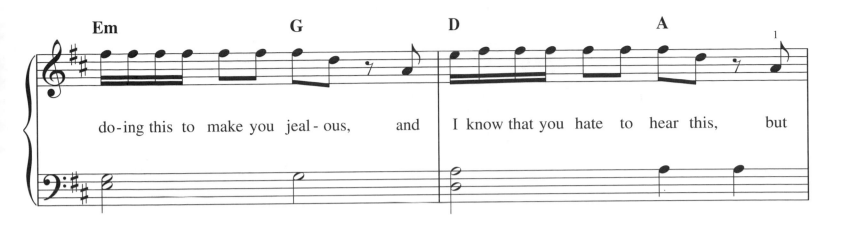

Em　　　　　　**G**　　　　　　**D**　　　　　　**A**

do-ing this to make you jeal-ous,　　and　　I know that you hate to hear this,　　but

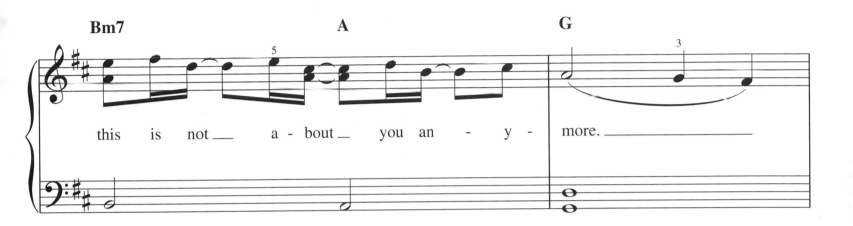

Bm7　　　　　　**A**　　　　　　**G**

this is not ___ a-bout ___ you an - y - more. ___

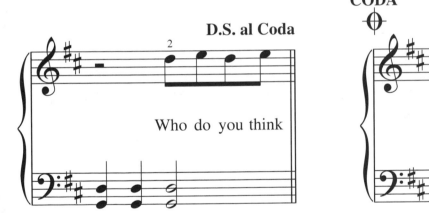

D.S. al Coda

Who do you think

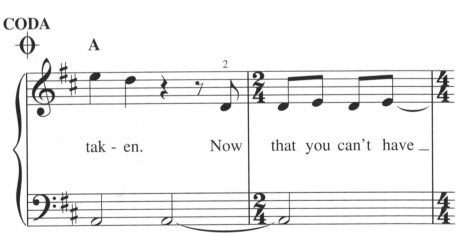

CODA　　　　**A**

tak - en.　　Now　that you can't have ___

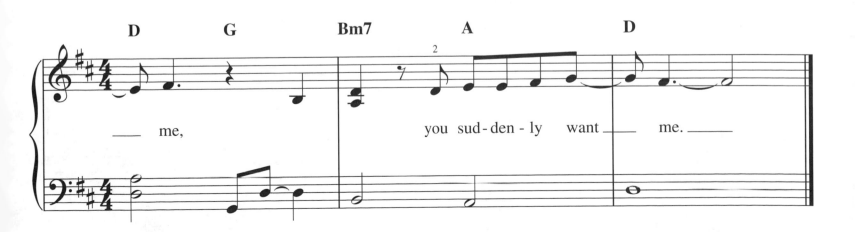

D　　**G**　　**Bm7**　　**A**　　**D**

___ me,　　you sud-den-ly want ___ me. ___

I WANT

Words and Music by
TOM FLETCHER

Am

You could be pre - oc - cu - pied, dif - f'rent date ev - 'ry night.
You've got ev - 'ry - thing you need, but you want ac - ces - so - ries;

F   **C**   **G/B**

You just got to say the word. ___ But
got to hold it say in your hand. ___

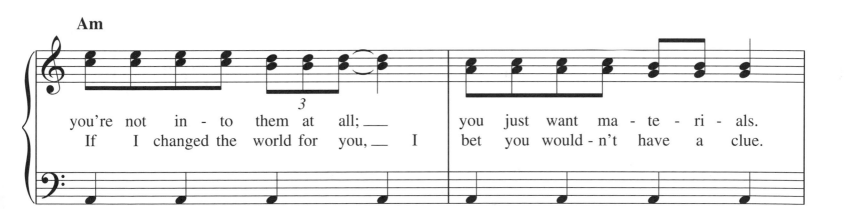

Am

you're not in - to them at all; ___ you just want ma - te - ri - als.
If I changed the world for you, ___ I bet you would - n't have a clue.

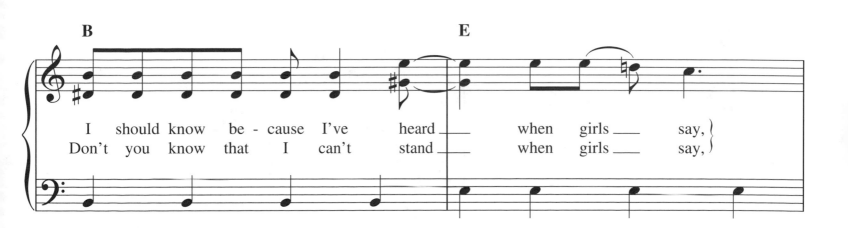

B   **E**

I should know be - cause I've heard ___ when girls ___ say,
Don't you know that I can't stand ___ when girls ___ say,

wan - na;   I'll   stay   true. _____   I   won - der   if   you

knew _____   what you   put   me   through. _   But   you want,   you want,   you   want _

_   me   to   love   you,   too. _____

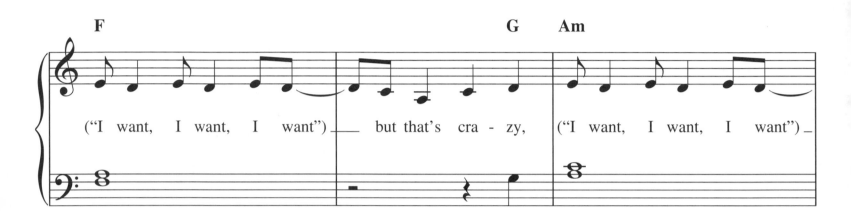

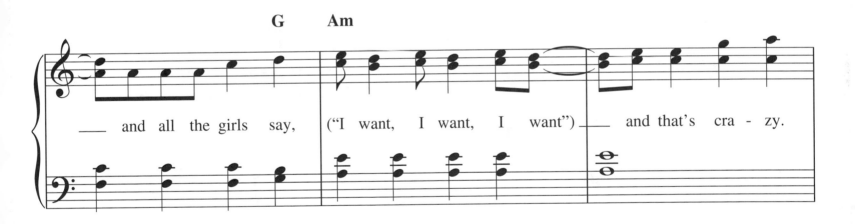

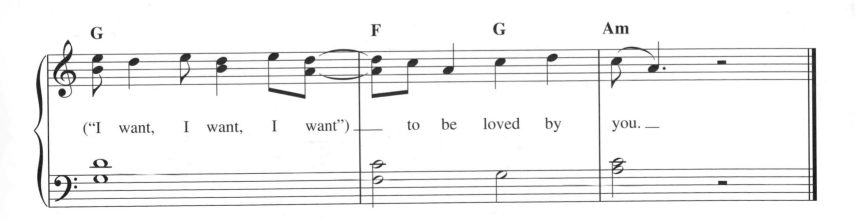

EVERYTHING ABOUT YOU

Words and Music by STEVE ROBSON,
WAYNE HECTOR, NIALL HORAN,
LIAM PAYNE, LOUIS TOMLINSON,
ZAIN MALIK and EDWARD STYLES

Dance tempo

You know I've al-ways got your back, girl, so let me be the one you come run-ning to,

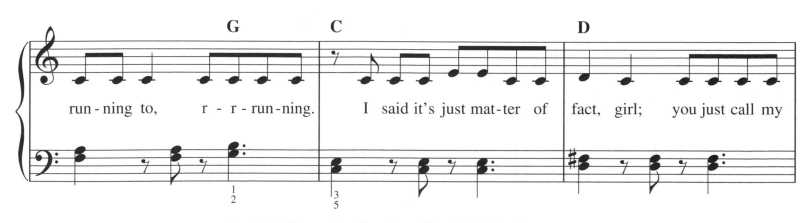

run-ning to, r - r - run-ning. I said it's just mat-ter of fact, girl; you just call my

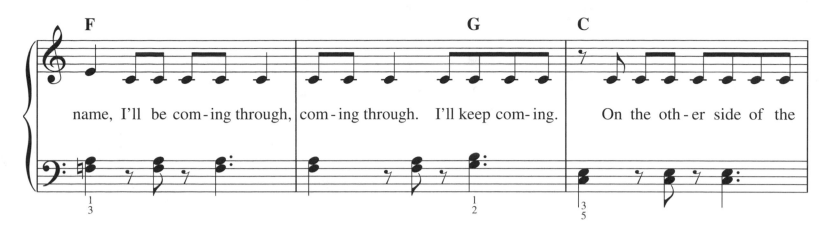

name, I'll be com-ing through, com-ing through. I'll keep com-ing. On the oth-er side of the

world, _ it don't mat-ter; I'll be there in two, I'll be there in two, I'll be there in two. _

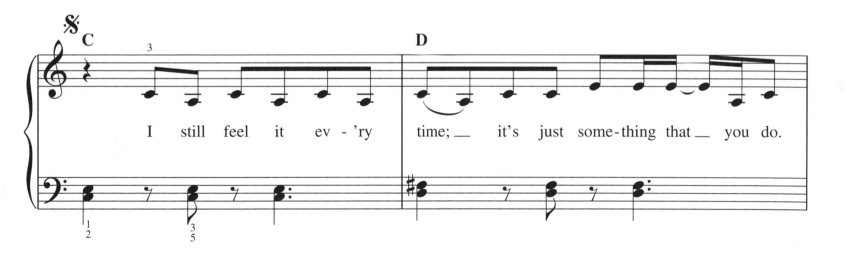

I still feel it ev-'ry time; _ it's just some-thing that _ you do.

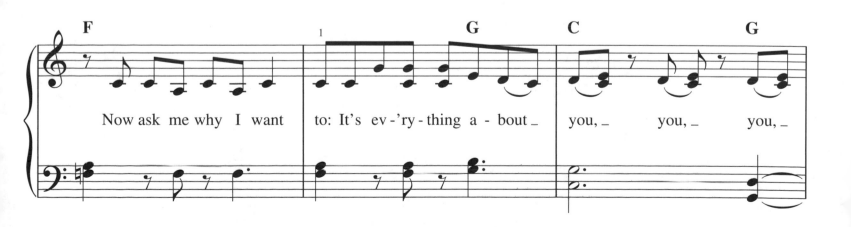

Now ask me why I want to: It's ev-'ry-thing a-bout _ you, _ you, _ you, _

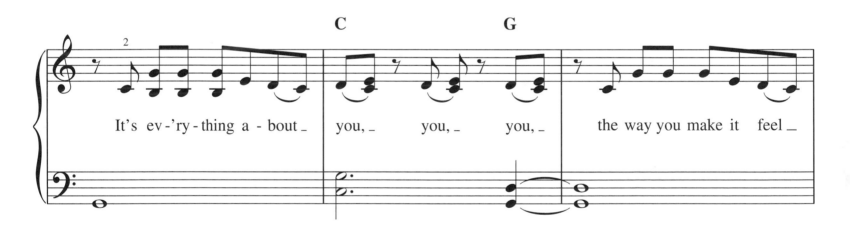

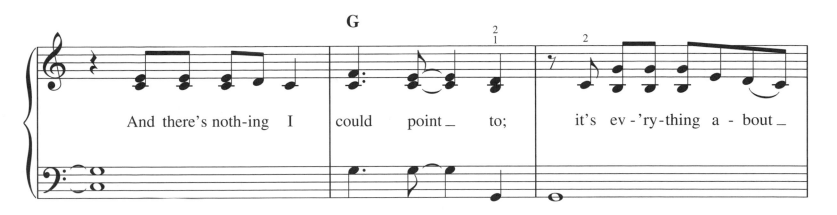

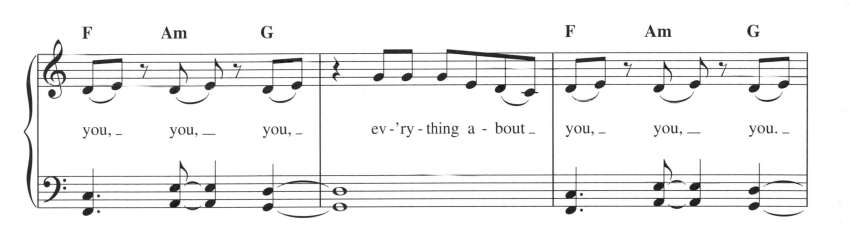

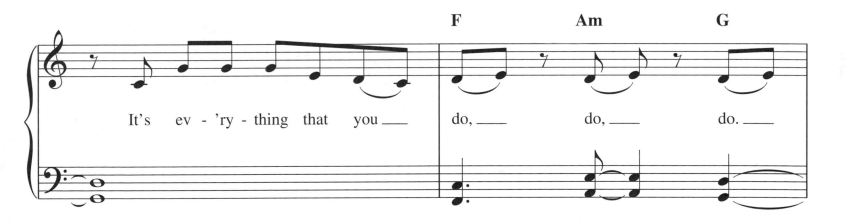

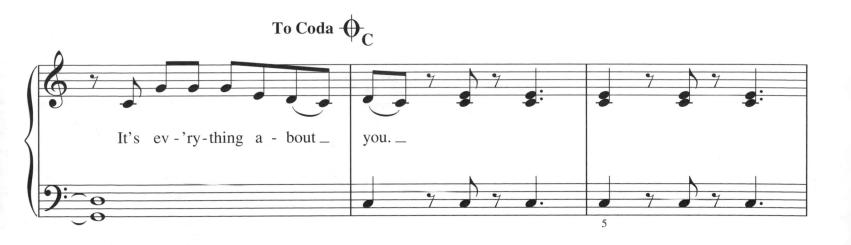

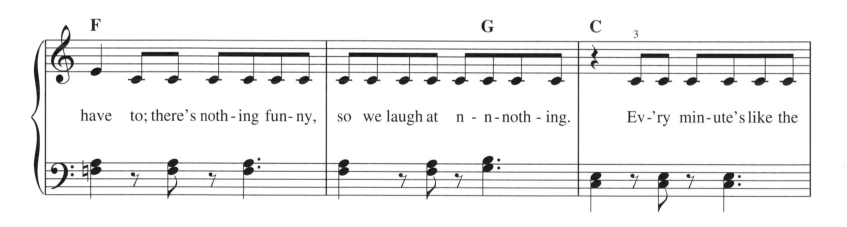

CODA

you. ___

And you have al - ways been the on - ly one I want - ed. And I

want - ed you to know: with - out you, I can't face it. ___ All we wan - na have is

fun, but they say that we're too young. Let them say what they

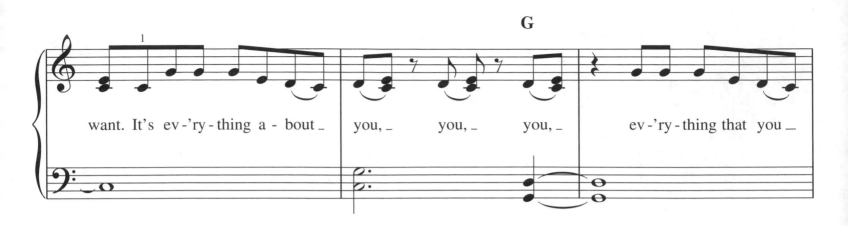

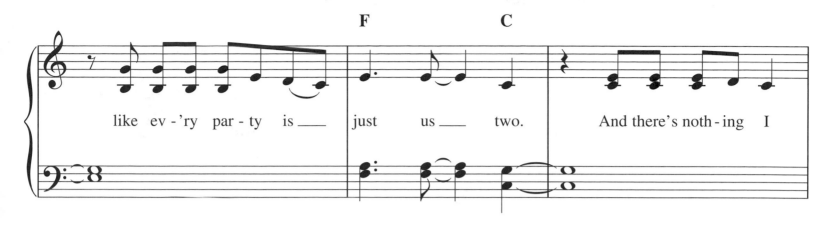

F   C

like ev-'ry par-ty is ___   just   us ___   two.   And there's noth-ing   I

G   F   Am   G

could   point ___   to;   it's ev-'ry-thing a - bout ___ you, ___   you, ___   you, ___

F   Am   G

ev-'ry-thing a - bout ___   you, ___   you, ___   you. ___   It's ev-'ry-thing that   you ___

F   Am   G   C

do, ___   do, ___   do. ___   It's ev-'ry-thing a - bout ___   you. ___

SAME MISTAKES

Words and Music by STEVE ROBSON,
WAYNE HECTOR, NIALL HORAN,
LIAM PAYNE, LOUIS TOMLINSON,
ZAIN MALIK and EDWARD STYLES

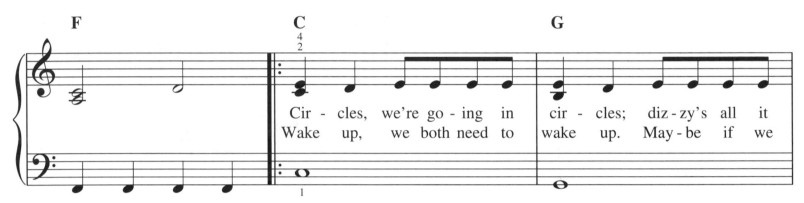

Cir - cles, we're go - ing in cir - cles; diz - zy's all it
Wake up, we both need to wake up. May - be if we

makes us. We know where it takes us; we've been be - fore. Clos - er, may - be look - ing
face up to ___ this, ___ we can make it through ___ this. Clos - er, may - be we'll be

clos - er; there's more to dis - cov - er, find out what went wrong with - out blam - ing each
clos - er, strong - er than we were be - fore, ___ yeah, make this some - thing more, ___ yeah.

oth - er. Think that we've got more time ___ when we're fall - ing be - hind. ___

___ Got - ta make up our minds, ___ or else we'll

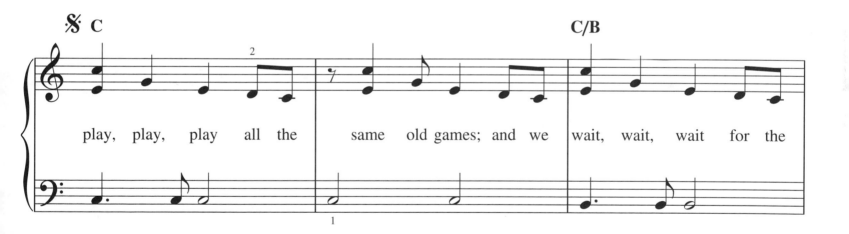

play, play, play all the same old games; and we wait, wait, wait for the

end to change; and we take, take, take it for grant-ed that we'll be the same. ___

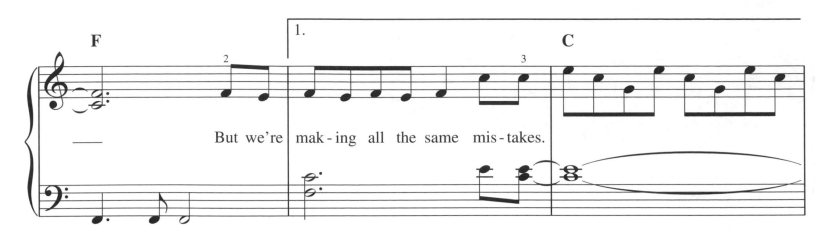

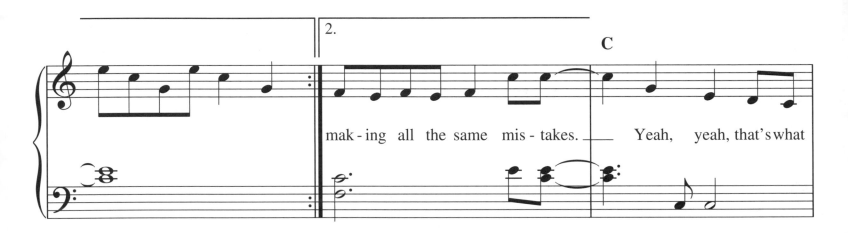

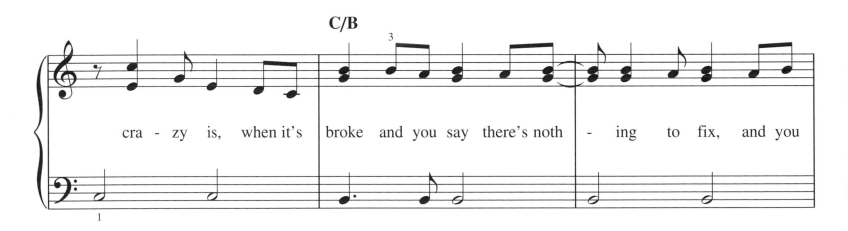

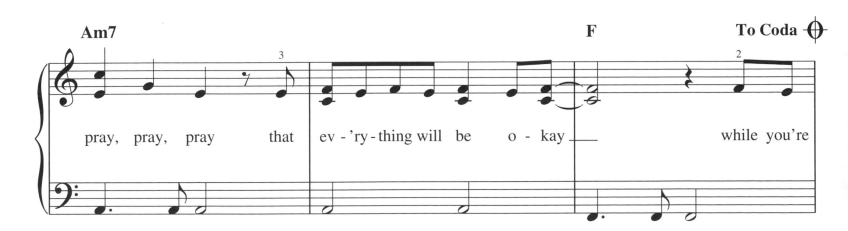

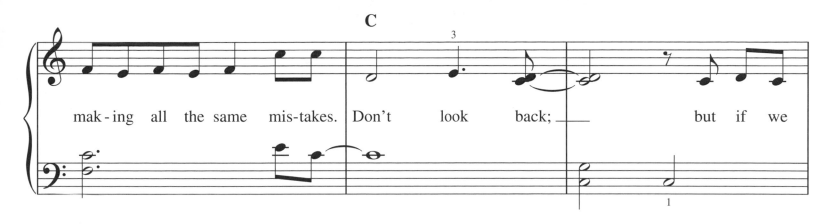

C

mak - ing all the same mis-takes. Don't look back; _____ but if we

Am   **Fmaj7**

don't look back, _____ we're on - ly learn - ing, babe, _____ how to

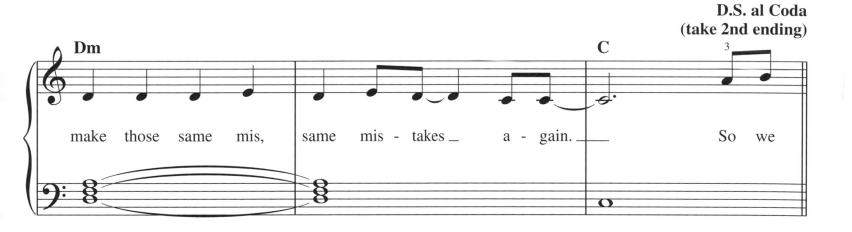

D.S. al Coda
(take 2nd ending)

Dm   **C**

make those same mis, same mis - takes _____ a - gain. _____ So we

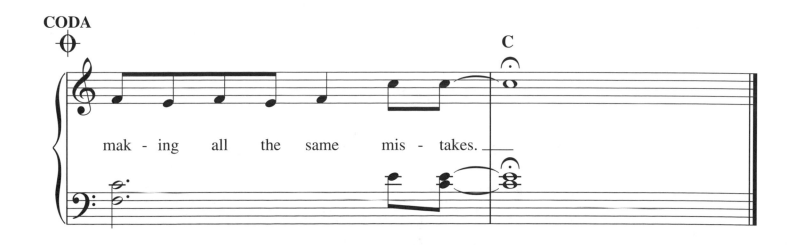

CODA

C

mak - ing all the same mis - takes. _____

SAVE YOU TONIGHT

Words and Music by SAVAN KOTECHA,
NADIR KHAYAT, JIMMY JOKER THORNFELDT,
GERALD SANDELL, ACHRAF JANNUSI,
BEATGEEK and ALAINA BEATON

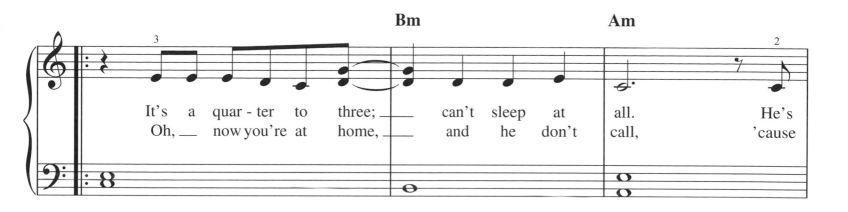

It's a quar-ter to three; ___ can't sleep at all. He's
Oh, ___ now you're at home, ___ and he don't call, 'cause

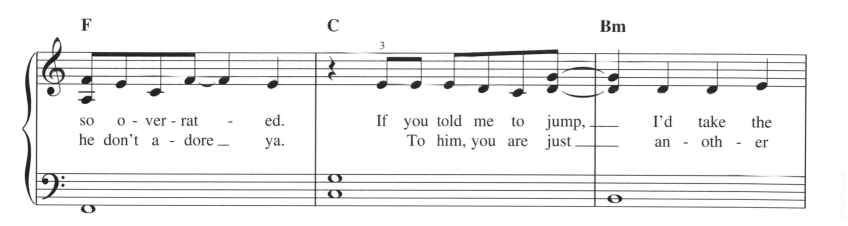

so o-ver-rat - ed. If you told me to jump, ___ I'd take the
he don't a-dore __ ya. To him, you are just ___ an-oth-er

fall, and he would-n't take __ it. All that you want's _
doll, and I tried to warn __ ya. What you want,what you need ___

___ un - der your nose, yeah. ___
___ has been right here, yeah. ___

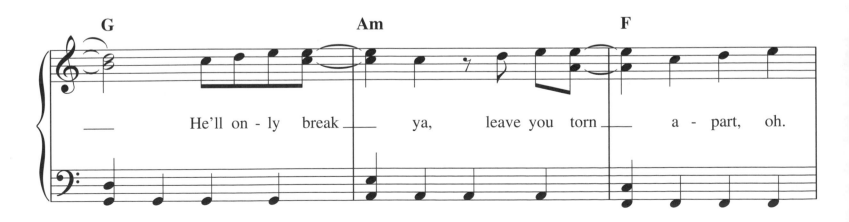

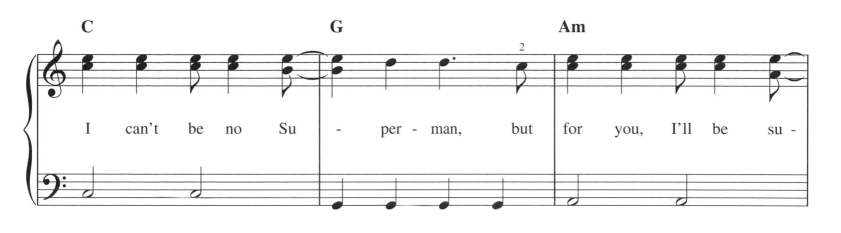

I can't be no Su - per - man, but for you, I'll be su -

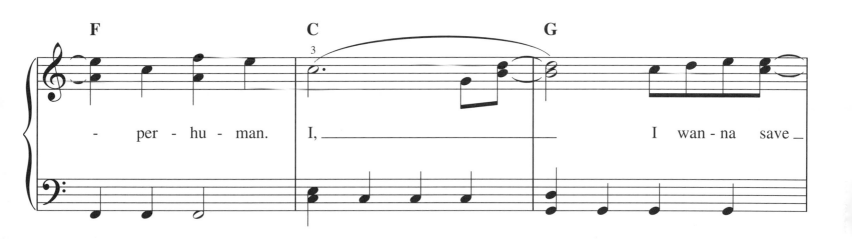

- per - hu - man. I, _____ I wan - na save _

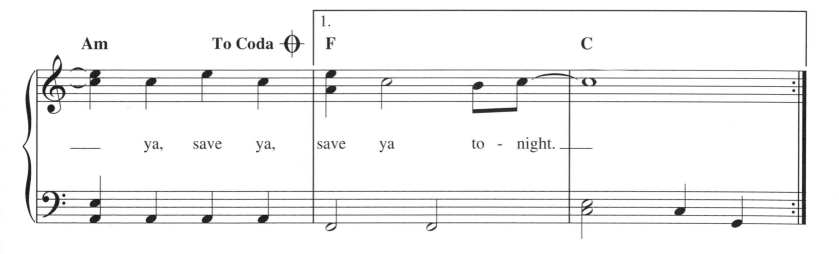

_ ya, save ya, save ya to - night. _ save ya to - night. _ Up, up _ and a - way, I'll

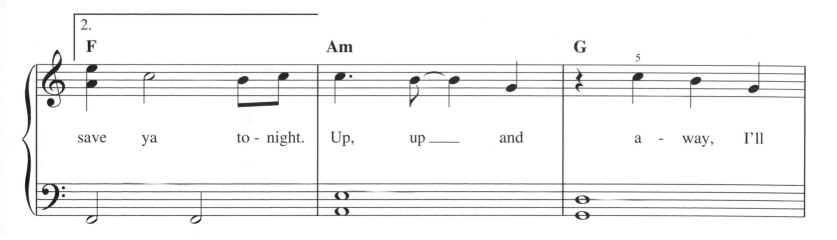

64

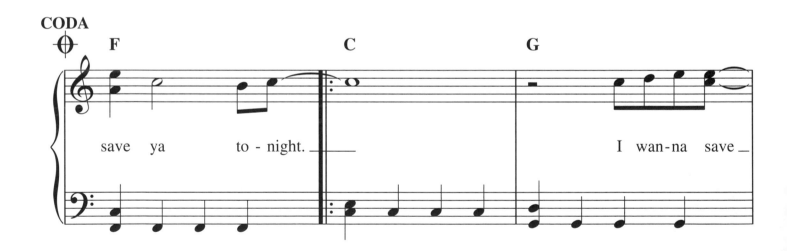

STOLE MY HEART

Words and Music by JAMIE SCOTT
and PAUL MEEHAN

The light shines; it's get-ting hot on my shoul-ders. _____

I don't mind; this time, it does-n't

mat - ter. _____ 'Cause your friends,

they look good, but you look bet - ter. _____

Don't you know, all night I've been wait-ing for a

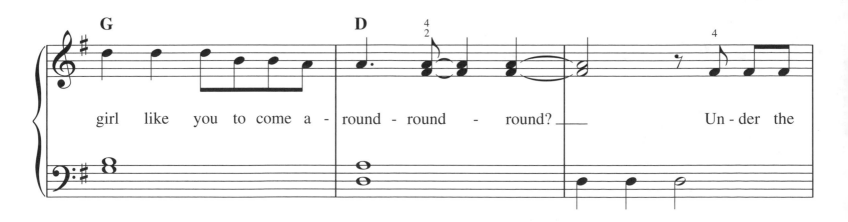

girl like you to come a - round - round - round? _____ Un - der the

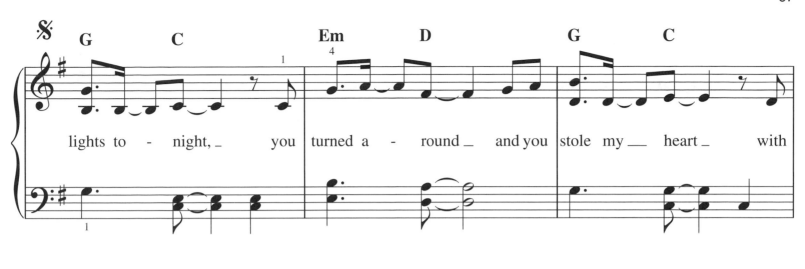

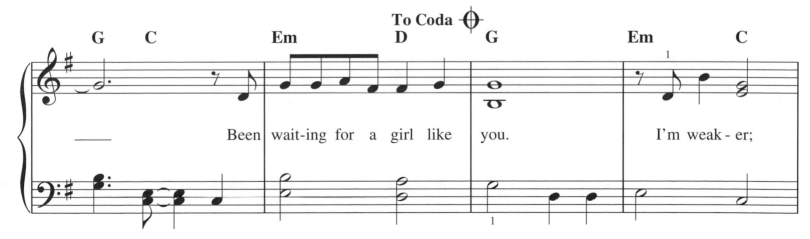

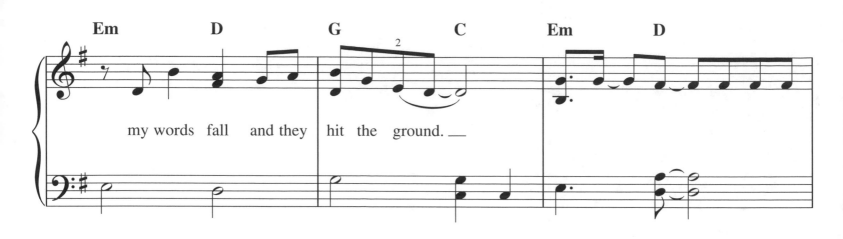

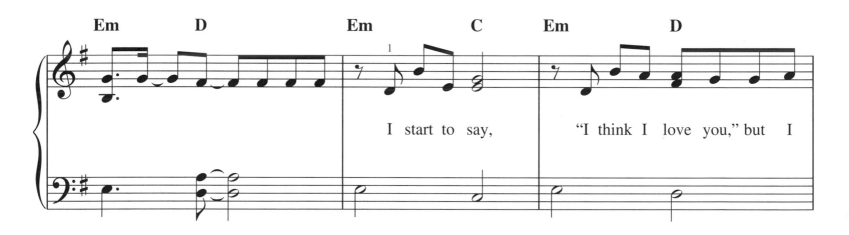

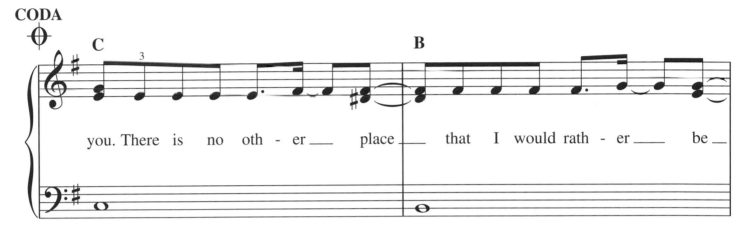

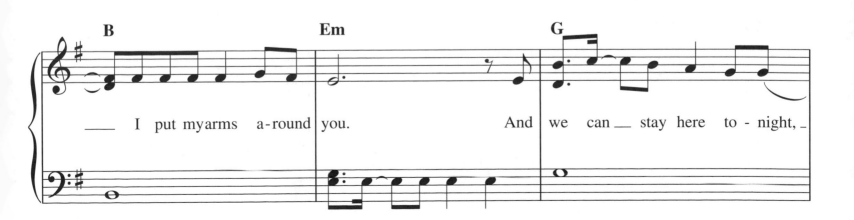

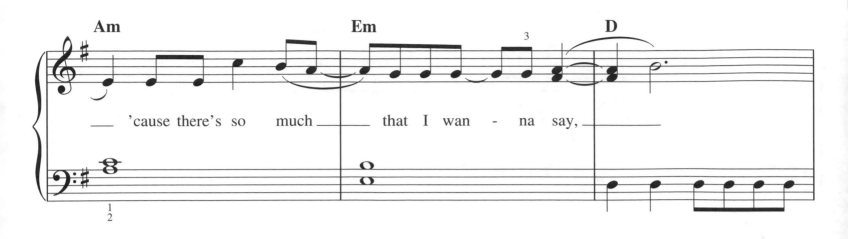

'cause there's so much ___ that I wan - na say, ___

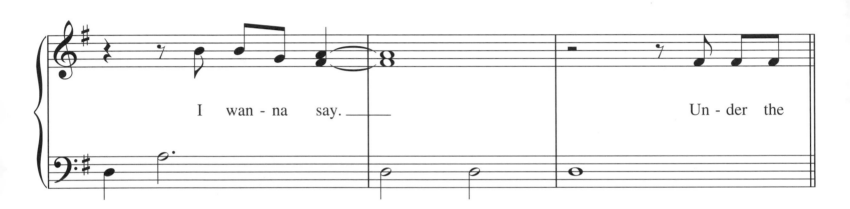

I wan - na say. ___ Un - der the

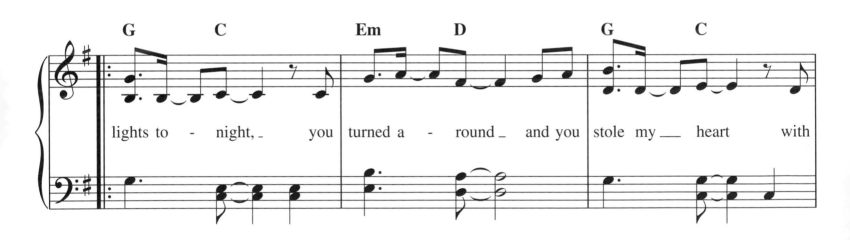

lights to - night, ___ you turned a - round ___ and you stole my ___ heart with

just one look. When I saw your ___ face, ___ I fell in ___ love. ___ It took a

min - ute, ___ girl, ___ to steal my heart. Un - der the steal my heart to - night. ___

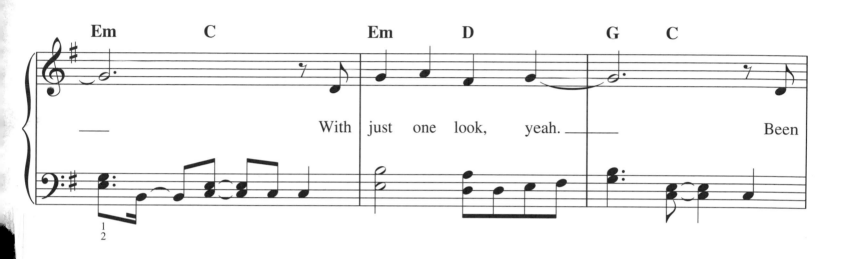

___ With just one look, yeah. ___ Been

wait-ing for a girl like you.

Been wait - ing for a girl like you.